BUDAPEST TRAVEL GUIDE 2023:
Experiencing The Danube Bend & Other Highlights Of Hungary (Beginner's Travel Guide)

Natalie R. Pate

Table Of Contents

WELCOME TO BUDAPEST

As I stepped off the plane at Budapest's Liszt Ferenc International Airport, I couldn't help but feel a sense of excitement and adventure coursing through my veins. I had always wanted to visit this beautiful and historic city, with its stunning architecture, rich culture, and delicious cuisine, and now, finally, I was here.

I made my way through the airport and onto the bustling streets of the city, taking in the sights and sounds around me. The air was crisp and cool, and the sun was shining bright in the clear blue sky. I hailed a taxi and soon found myself on my way to my hotel, located in the heart of the city.

As we drove through the winding streets, I couldn't help but feel a sense of awe at the sheer beauty of the place. The buildings were stunning, with their intricate facades and ornate details, and the streets were alive with people going about their daily business. I was struck by the vibrant energy of the city, and couldn't wait to explore it further.

Finally, we arrived at my hotel, a beautiful old building with high ceilings and ornate chandeliers. I checked in and made my way to my room, where I unpacked and freshened up before heading out to explore the city.

I decided to start my visit with a tour of the famous Buda Castle, located on the Buda side of the Danube River. The castle, which dates back to the 13th century, was a true marvel of architectural beauty, with its grand halls, beautiful gardens, and stunning views of the city below. I spent hours wandering the castle's many corridors and rooms, taking in the rich history and culture of the place.

After my visit to the castle, I made my way to the Gellért Thermal Baths, located in the Gellért Hotel.

The baths, which are fed by natural thermal springs, are a true oasis of relaxation and rejuvenation, and I spent hours soaking in the warm, soothing waters.

As the day turned to evening, I decided to grab a bite to eat at one of the city's many quaint and charming cafes. I chose a small, family-owned establishment that served traditional Hungarian cuisine, and was treated to a delicious meal of goulash, dumplings, and a crisp, refreshing glass of white wine.

As I enjoyed my meal, I couldn't help but feel a sense of gratitude and appreciation for this beautiful city and the wonderful people who called it home. I knew that my visit to Budapest was just beginning, and I couldn't wait to see what other adventures and experiences this amazing place had in store for me.

The next day, I set out to explore more of the city. I started my day with a visit to the Great Market Hall, a bustling indoor market that was filled with stalls selling a wide variety of goods, from fresh produce and spices to handmade crafts and souvenirs. I spent hours wandering the market, chatting with the friendly vendors and sampling some of the delicious local specialties.

After my visit to the market, I decided to take a walk along the Danube River and see some of the city's iconic landmarks. I made my way to the Chain Bridge, which connects the Buda and Pest sides of the city, and took in the stunning views of the river and the city skyline.

I also stopped by the Hungarian Parliament Building, a stunning neo-Gothic structure that is one of the tallest and most impressive buildings in Budapest. I was in awe of its grandeur and history, and spent some time taking photos and soaking up the atmosphere.

As the day drew to a close, I decided to visit one of the city's many thermal baths for a relaxing evening soak. I chose the Széchenyi Thermal Bath, which is the largest and most popular bath in Budapest. The bath, which is fed by natural thermal springs, was a true oasis of relaxation, with its warm, soothing waters and beautiful surroundings.

After my soak, I headed back to my hotel, feeling rejuvenated and refreshed. I knew that I had only scratched the surface of all that Budapest had to offer, and I couldn't wait to see what other adventures and experiences the city had in store for me.

Over the next few days, I continued to explore the city and all that it had to offer. I visited the beautiful St. Stephen's Basilica, took a leisurely stroll through the city's many parks and gardens, and sampled some of the delicious local cuisine.

I also made a point to visit some of the city's many museums and cultural attractions, including the Hungarian National Gallery and the House of Terror, which is dedicated to the history of the country's communist regime.

But perhaps the highlight of my trip was my visit to the Széchenyi Chain Bridge, a stunning 19th-century bridge that spans the Danube River and connects the Buda and Pest sides of the city. The bridge, which is illuminated at night, was absolutely breathtaking, and I spent hours just walking along it and taking in the views.

As my trip came to an end, I couldn't help but feel a sense of sadness at the thought of leaving this beautiful city. I knew that my visit to Budapest had been an unforgettable experience, one that I would always cherish. And I knew that I would have to come back someday, to explore even more of this amazing place and all that it had to offer.

History

Budapest is the capital and largest city of Hungary, a country located in Central Europe. The city is located on the banks of the Danube River, which divides the city into two parts: Buda, on the western side of the river, and Pest, on the eastern side. The city has a rich history that dates back to the Roman Empire and has been a major cultural, political, and economic center for centuries.

The first settlement in the area that is now Budapest was established by the Celts in the 9th century BC. The Romans later conquered the region and established a military camp called Aquincum in the

1st century AD. Aquincum later became a major city in the Roman Empire and was an important center of trade and commerce.

After the fall of the Roman Empire, the city came under the control of various European powers, including the Magyars, who arrived in the 9th century and established their own kingdom. In the Middle Ages, the city was an important cultural and political center and was home to many universities, libraries, and cultural institutions.

In the 19th century, the city underwent significant modernization and industrialization and became an important hub for trade and transportation. It was also a center of political and cultural activity and was home to many artists, writers, and intellectuals.

In the 20th century, Budapest played a significant role in European history. It was the site of several important events, including the 1956 Hungarian Revolution, which led to the fall of the Soviet Union's influence in the country. Today, Budapest is a thriving metropolis with a rich history, vibrant culture, and a thriving economy. It is a popular destination for tourists from around the world, who come to see its many historical landmarks, cultural institutions, and natural beauty

CHAPTER 1: VISA PROCCESSING

If you're planning a trip to Budapest, you may be wondering what the visa process is like. In this book, we'll provide an overview of the visa process for tourists visiting Budapest, including what types of visas are available, how to apply for a visa, and what documents you'll need to provide.

What types of visas are available for tourists visiting Budapest?

There are two main types of visas available for tourists visiting Budapest: short-stay visas and long-stay visas.

Short-stay visas, also known as Schengen visas, allow you to stay in Budapest for up to 90 days within a 180-day period. These visas are suitable for tourists who are planning a short trip to Budapest, such as a holiday or a business trip.

Long-stay visas, also known as national visas, allow you to stay in Budapest for more than 90 days. These visas are suitable for tourists who are planning a longer stay in Budapest, such as studying or working in the city.

Which type of visa do I need to visit Budapest?

The type of visa you'll need to visit Budapest depends on the length of your stay. If you're planning a short trip to Budapest, a short-stay visa (Schengen visa) is sufficient. If you're planning a longer stay in Budapest, such as for study or work, you'll need a long-stay visa (national visa).

How do I apply for a visa to visit Budapest?

The process for applying for a visa to visit Budapest varies depending on your country of origin and the type of visa you need. Here are the general steps you'll need to follow to apply for a visa to visit Budapest:

1. **Determine which type of visa you need:** As mentioned above, you'll need to determine whether you need a short-stay visa (Schengen visa) or a long-stay visa (national visa) based on the length of your stay in Budapest.

2. **Check if you need to apply for a visa:** If you're a citizen of an EU member state, you don't

need a visa to visit Budapest. However, if you're a citizen of a non-EU country, you'll need to apply for a visa. You can check the list of countries that require a visa to visit Hungary on the Hungarian Ministry of Foreign Affairs website.

3. **Choose the right embassy or consulate:** Depending on where you live, you'll need to apply for a visa at the Hungarian embassy or consulate in your country. You can find a list of Hungarian embassies and consulates on the Hungarian Ministry of Foreign Affairs website.

4. **Gather the required documents:** To apply for a visa, you'll need to provide a number of documents, including your passport, a completed visa application form, and proof of

your travel plans (such as a round-trip ticket and hotel reservation). You may also need to provide proof of your financial means (such as a bank statement), and proof of your health insurance coverage.

5. **Submit your application:** Once you have all the required documents, you'll need to submit your application in person at the Hungarian embassy or consulate in your country. You may also be required to pay a visa fee at this time.

6. **Wait for a decision:** After you submit your application, it will be processed by the Hungarian embassy or consulate. This process can take several weeks, so be sure to apply for your visa well in advance of your trip.

to provide to apply for a visa to visit Budapest will depend on the type of visa you're applying for and your individual circumstances. However, here are some documents that you'll generally need to provide:

- **Passport:** You'll need to provide a valid passport with at least two blank pages. Your passport should also be valid for at least three months beyond the end of your planned stay in Budapest.

- **Visa application form:** You'll need to complete a visa application form and submit it along with your other documents. You can download the application form from the Hungarian Ministry of Foreign Affairs website.

- **Passport-sized photograph:** You'll need to provide a passport-sized photograph that meets the required specifications.

- **Proof of travel plans:** You'll need to provide proof of your travel plans, such as a round-trip ticket and hotel reservation.

- **Proof of financial means:** You'll need to provide proof of your financial means, such as a bank statement, to show that you have sufficient funds to cover your expenses during your stay in Budapest.

- **Health insurance:** You'll need to provide proof of health insurance coverage for your stay in Budapest.

- **Other documents:** Depending on your individual circumstances, you may need to provide additional documents, such as a letter of invitation from a host in Hungary or a certificate of employment.

It's important to note that the visa process can be complex, and the requirements may vary depending on your country of origin and the type of visa you're applying for. Be sure to check the specific requirements for your situation on the Hungarian Ministry of Foreign Affairs website, and allow plenty of time to gather all the necessary documents and submit your application.

What is the cost of a visa to visit Budapest?

The cost of a visa to visit Budapest depends on the type of visa you're applying for and your country of origin. For short-stay visas (Schengen visas), the fee is generally around 80 EUR. For long-stay visas (national visas), the fee is generally around 100 EUR. However, these fees may vary, so it's best to check the current fee schedule on the Hungarian Ministry of Foreign Affairs website.

In addition to the visa fee, you may also need to pay a service fee to the embassy or consulate handling your application. This fee may be paid in cash or by credit card.

Can I apply for a visa online?

In some cases, you may be able to apply for a visa online through the Hungarian e-Visa portal. This portal allows you to apply for a short-stay visa (Schengen visa) online and pay the visa fee electronically. However, not all countries are eligible for the e-Visa service, so it's important to check the list of eligible countries on the Hungarian Ministry of Foreign Affairs website.

If you're eligible for the e-Visa service, you'll still need to gather the required documents and submit them online as part of your application. You may also be required to appear in person at a Hungarian embassy or consulate to provide biometric data (such as fingerprints) and have your passport and visa issued.

How long does it take to process a visa application?

The processing time for a visa application to visit Budapest varies depending on the type of visa you're applying for and your individual circumstances. However, it's generally recommended to apply for your visa at least two months before your planned trip to allow plenty of time for the application process.

For short-stay visas (Schengen visas), the processing time is generally around 15 calendar days. For long-stay visas (national visas), the processing time can be longer, up to 60 calendar days.

However, it's important to note that the processing time may be longer during peak travel seasons or if additional documentation is required.

What if my visa application is denied?

If your visa application is denied, you'll receive a written notification explaining the reasons for the decision. In some cases, you may be able to appeal the decision or reapply for a visa. If you're unsure about the reasons for the denial or how to proceed, it's recommended to contact the Hungarian embassy or consulate handling your application for further information.

Tips for a successful visa application

To increase your chances of a successful visa application to visit Budapest, here are a few tips to keep in mind:

1. **Apply well in advance:** As mentioned above, it's generally recommended to apply for your visa at least two months before your planned trip to allow plenty of time for the application process.

2. **Gather all the required documents:** Be sure to gather all the required documents before submitting your application. This includes your passport, completed visa application form, and any other documents required by the embassy or consulate.

3. **Double-check your application:** Make sure to double-check your application for errors or incomplete information before submitting it. This will help ensure that your application is processed smoothly and efficiently.

4. **Follow the embassy or consulate's instructions:** Be sure to follow all the instructions provided by the embassy or consulate handling your application. This includes appearing in person for biometric data collection and passport issuance if required.

5. **Stay organized:** Keep all your documents and receipts organized and in a safe place. This will make it easier to provide any additional information or documentation if needed.

The visa process for tourists visiting Budapest can be complex, but by following the steps outlined in this book and gathering all the required documents, you can increase your chances of a successful application. It's important to allow plenty of time for the application process and to follow the instructions provided by the embassy or consulate handling your application. With proper planning and organization, you can be on your way to enjoying all that Budapest has to offer.

CHAPT 2: CITY OF BUDAPEST

 The city is known for its stunning architecture, thermal baths, and delicious cuisine, but there is much more to its story than just these modern-day attractions.

The city was founded in the year 896 by the Magyars, a group of nomadic tribes who had settled in the region. It was originally called Buda, after the name of the region, and it was a small fortification built on the banks of the Danube river.

Over the centuries, Buda grew into a thriving city, and in the 13th century, King Béla IV established it as the capital of Hungary. The city continued to grow and prosper, and in the 19th century, it became a hub for industry and trade. It was during this time that the city merged with the neighboring city of Pest, which was located on the opposite side of the Danube. Together, the two cities formed the modern-day metropolis of Budapest.

Today, Budapest is a vibrant and cosmopolitan city, with a population of over 1.7 million people. It is a hub of culture and arts, with numerous museums, galleries, and theaters. It is also home to some of the most beautiful architecture in Europe, with a mix of medieval castles, baroque palaces, and Art Nouveau buildings.

One of the most iconic landmarks in Budapest is Buda Castle, which sits atop Castle Hill and offers breathtaking views of the city. The castle was originally built in the 13th century and has undergone numerous renovations and expansions over the years. Today, it is home to the Hungarian National Gallery and the Budapest History Museum.

In addition to its cultural and historical attractions, Budapest is also known for its thermal baths. The city has a number of thermal baths, which are fed by natural hot springs that are rich in minerals. These baths are a popular destination for tourists and locals alike, and are a great way to relax and rejuvenate after a long day of sightseeing.

Overall, Budapest is a city with a rich and diverse history that is waiting to be explored. Whether you are interested in its cultural attractions, its stunning architecture, or its thermal baths, there is something for everyone in this vibrant and dynamic city. So, it is a must-visit destination for any traveler.

Getting to Budapest and getting around

As a tourist, one of the first things you will need to figure out is how to get around the city. Here are some options for getting around Budapest:

Public Transportation: Budapest has an extensive public transportation system, including buses, trams, and metro trains. The metro is the most efficient way to get around the city, with three lines that cover most of the major attractions. You can purchase a single ticket or a multi-day pass at any metro station, and tickets are valid for all forms of public transportation. Keep in mind that tickets must be validated before you board.

Taxis: Taxis are widely available in Budapest, and they can be a convenient option for getting around the city. However, it is important to be cautious when using taxis, as there have been reports of scams and overcharging. To avoid these issues, it is best to use a reputable taxi company or to hail a taxi from the street rather than booking one through a hotel or restaurant. It is also a good idea to agree on the fare before getting in the taxi.

Bicycles: Budapest is a bike-friendly city, with numerous bike lanes and rental stations throughout the city. Renting a bike is a great way to get around and explore the city at your own pace. There are several companies that offer bike rentals, and you can usually find a station near popular tourist attractions.

Walking: Budapest is a very walkable city, and many of the major attractions are within walking distance of each other. Strolling through the city is a great way to discover hidden gems and get a feel for the local culture. Just be sure to wear comfortable shoes and stay safe by following basic pedestrian rules.

Boat Tours: One unique way to see the city is by taking a boat tour along the Danube River. There are several companies that offer tours, ranging from short sightseeing cruises to longer dinner cruises. This is a great option for getting a different perspective on the city and seeing some of the landmarks from the water.

There are several options for getting around Budapest. The public transportation system is efficient and affordable, but taxis and bike rentals can also be convenient. Walking and boat tours are great ways to see the city and explore at your own pace. Whatever mode of transportation you choose, be sure to plan ahead and stay safe while exploring this beautiful city.

CHAPTER 3: BUDGETING AND PLANNING

Budapest's popularity among visitors is largely due to its reputation as a low-cost destination. Many tourists still think it's less expensive than other European capitals, despite the fact that prices have risen over the years.

Here are some practical advice for stretching your Budapest dollars further.

Budapest's primary airport is served by low-cost airlines.

Budapest only has one airport, unlike many major European cities that have separate remote airports for low-cost airlines. You will arrive at the same location whether you fly in on a flagship airline or a low-cost carrier. Budapest Airport is the home base for the Hungarian low-cost carrier WIZZ Air.

From the airport, take public transportation into Budapest.

Budapest's airport is technically part of the city, but it's a long way from the action, so you'll need to arrange for a transfer. Thankfully, there is reasonably priced public transportation to get you where you need to go. You can either get off at Kalvin tér for metro line 4 or Deák Ferenc tér for metro lines 1, 2, and 3. A one-way bus 100E ticket to the city costs 900 HUF (roughly $3 US). You are in the center of downtown Pest from either stop.

With our weekly newsletter, you can receive more travel ideas, advice, and special deals delivered right to your inbox.

Instead of taking a tour bus, use public transportation to explore the city.

Want to take a sightseeing bus trip at a much lower cost? Take the Budapest transit system. One of the most picturesque tram lines is tram line 2, which travels north to south along the Danube. Along the way, you'll see the entire Pest side of the riverbanks of the Danube as well as breathtaking views of Castle Hill and the Hungarian Parliament.

Take trams 19 or 41 to go to the Danube's riverbanks on the Buda side. Alternatively, you may board bus 105 above ground, which will take you to Heroes' Square and back along the Danube, along Andrássy Avenue, a Unesco-listed avenue. A single bus fare costs just 350 HUF (about $1).

Hostels are abundant in Budapest's center.

Budapest has a ton of fantastic hostels, so it's simple to locate a dorm or a cheap private room in the heart of the city. Dorms may be found for as little as

$8 per night, but if you want to sleep well, stay away from "party hostels."

There are other inexpensive lodging options in the VIII, IX, and XI districts.

There are also inexpensive hotels in Budapest that are not hostels, and they grow more affordable the more you go from the city center. Try the artistic VIII District, the IX District in Pest, or the XI District in Buda if you're looking for a lively, affordable neighborhood close to the center. Avoid areas that can be seedy at night by staying inside the Grand Boulevard (Nagykört) ring.

Find a homestay or couchsurf to stay with locals.

Instead of renting out a full space or booking a hotel room, choose a homestay or a room in an apartment to get a more intimate - and less costly - experience of Budapest. You can find private rooms with local hosts on Airbnb (be sure to carefully read the ratings and reviews), homestays on Homestay.com, and occasionally on Booking.com. Another possibility is couch surfing. You may ask local group members in the Budapest "Official" Couchsurfing group for hosting or guidance.

The Danube in the summer with public transportation

You must sail the Danube if you visit Budapest in the summer. The greatest way to see Budapest's most well-known attractions, including Buda Castle, the Hungarian Parliament, and the bridges, is from the river.

But you may use the boat run by BKK, Budapest's local transportation company, instead of booking an expensive Danube tour. One of these trips costs 750 HUF (just over $2) per person. Only during the summer are boat services available, therefore check the BKK website for departure hours.

Select the straightforward, less-touristy thermal baths.

Budapest is well-known for its ancient thermal baths, but if you don't want to spend $20, check out the less well-known spas. Tickets for the basic and inexpensive Dandár Baths in the XI District cost 2800 HUF, or slightly under $10. However, you may still visit the well-known baths on a tight budget if you go to the Lukács Baths after 5 p.m., when admission is just 2600 HUF rather than 3500 HUF.

Go to Budapest in the spring or the autumn.

In addition to being more affordable, spring and autumn are the most lovely seasons of year to visit Budapest. In the spring, the flowers of the fruit trees give the city a vibrant hue, while in the autumn, Budapest takes on a lovely shade of rust.

In addition to being beautiful in nature, these shoulder seasons are also easy on the pocketbook. Avoid the summer, particularly August, if you're trying to save money on **accommodations.** Prices might soar during this time, especially if you're traveling during the Sziget Festival or the Formula 1 Grand Prix. Another busy month that might raise costs is December, when the Christmas markets are in full flow.

Purchase lunch from nearby markets or dine from the restaurant's daily menu.

Try the food courts in the market halls, like the one in Nagycsarnok, if you're on a tight budget; they're less costly than dining at sit-down restaurants. The market booths are a fantastic spot to stock up on ingredients for a picnic if you want to prepare your own food. However, if you still feel like eating out, you may do it on a budget by keeping an eye out for lunch menus. Even at more tourist-oriented downtown restaurants, a two- or three-course lunch menu (ebéd menü) is commonly available for US$10–$15.

Purchase a Budapest Card to get discounts on transit and museum admission.

Look into the Budapest Card if you want to utilize public transportation and visit the city's key tourist destinations, including the Hungarian National Museum, Ludwig Museum, Memento Park, and Museum of Fine Arts. A cave tour, free public transportation, free admission to 20 museums, the Lukács Baths, and special rates for excursions and restaurants are all included with the Budapest Card. A 24-hour card costs US$25; 48 hours are available for US$37; and 72 hours are available for US$49. As you plan your vacation, do the arithmetic to see if the Budapest Card will result in cost savings.

Budapest offers discounts to retirees and students from throughout Europe

When presenting their ID, residents of the European Economic Area are entitled to discounts at places like the Hungarian Parliament. Visitors under the age of 26 and EEA citizens 62 to 70 are eligible for discounted museum admission (over 70s are admitted free). The use of public transit is likewise free for EU citizens over 65.

Play Movie

Welcome to Budapest

Costs of living in Budapest

Dorm room bed at a hostel: 2600-8100 HUF

11,000–32,500 HUF for a standard hotel room for two.

Self-catering apartment: starting at 14,500 HUF (including Airbnb).

24-hour public transportation pass: 1650 HUF

400–1200 HUF for coffee

2000–6000 HUF for a sandwich

Two-person dinner: 8000–25,000 HUF

At the bar, a beer costs 600–1200 HUF.

CHAPTER 4: ACCOMMODATION

Options For Hotels:

Budapest is a vibrant and cosmopolitan city that attracts millions of travelers each year. With its rich history, stunning architecture, and delicious cuisine, it's no wonder that Budapest is such a popular destination. When it comes to finding the perfect hotel, there are a range of options to suit all budgets and preferences. Here are some great options to consider when planning your trip to Budapest:

Four Seasons Hotel Gresham Palace: Located in the heart of the city, this luxurious hotel is housed in a stunning Art Nouveau building that dates back to 1906. It offers breathtaking views of the Danube River and the Buda Castle, as well as elegant rooms and suites that are tastefully decorated in a classic style. The Four Seasons also boasts a spa and fitness center, making it the perfect choice for travelers who want to indulge in some pampering.

Hotel Rum: This trendy hotel is located in the trendy district of Belváros-Lipótváros and offers a unique blend of vintage and modern design. It features a rooftop bar with panoramic views of the city, as well as a restaurant serving delicious Hungarian cuisine. The Hotel Rum is a great option for travelers who want to be at the center of the action and enjoy the city's vibrant nightlife.

Boutique Hotel Victoria: If you're looking for something a bit more intimate and personal, the Boutique Hotel Victoria might be just what you're looking for. Located in the historic district of Buda, this charming hotel offers a cozy atmosphere and beautifully decorated rooms and suites. It also boasts a spa and a restaurant serving international cuisine. The Boutique Hotel Victoria is ideal for travelers who want to relax and unwind in a more peaceful setting.

Hotel Palazzo Zichy: This grand hotel is located in the vibrant district of Újbuda and features beautiful Art Nouveau architecture. It offers spacious rooms and suites, a spa, and a rooftop bar with stunning views of the city. The Hotel Palazzo Zichy is a great choice for travelers who want to experience the grandeur of the city and enjoy all that it has to offer.

Option For Hostels:

The Little Hostel: Located in the heart of the city, The Little Hostel offers a warm and welcoming atmosphere at an affordable price. It features private and shared rooms, as well as a common area where you can socialize with other travelers. The

Little Hostel also offers a range of activities, such as guided city tours and cooking classes, to help you make the most of your stay.

The Nest Hostel: This popular hostel is located in the trendy district of Belváros-Lipótváros and offers a mix of private and shared rooms. It features a rooftop terrace with panoramic views of the city, as well as a bar and a common area where you can relax and socialize. The Nest Hostel is a great option for travelers who want to be at the center of the action and enjoy the city's vibrant nightlife.

Hostel One Home: Located in the historic district of Buda, this stylish hostel offers a range of private and shared rooms. It features a common area with a fireplace, a fully equipped kitchen, and a terrace where you can sit and relax. Hostel One Home is ideal for travelers who want a more peaceful and homely atmosphere.

The Sleeping Camel: This quirky hostel is located in the vibrant district of Újbuda and offers a range of private and shared rooms. It features a common area with a bar and a garden where you can sit and relax. The Sleeping Camel is a great choice for travelers who want a more laid-back and fun atmosphere.

Option For Vacation Rentals:

Luxurious apartments: If you're looking for something extra special, consider staying in one of Budapest's luxurious apartments. These spacious and stylish rentals offer all the amenities you need to feel right at home, including fully equipped kitchens, comfortable bedrooms, and modern bathrooms. Many of these apartments also feature balconies or terraces with stunning views of the city.

Cozy apartments: For a more intimate and homely atmosphere, consider staying in one of Budapest's cozy apartments. These rentals are typically smaller and more modestly decorated, but they offer all the amenities you need for a comfortable stay. They are ideal for travelers who want to experience the local way of life and immerse themselves in the city's rich culture.

Family-friendly rentals: If you're traveling with children, you'll want to find a rental that is suitable for families. There are many vacation rentals in Budapest that offer extra space and amenities for families, such as children's bedrooms, play areas, and outdoor spaces. These rentals are ideal for travelers who want to spend quality time together and create lasting memories.

Pet-friendly rentals: If you're traveling with your furry friend, you'll want to find a rental that is pet-friendly. There are many vacation rentals in

Budapest that welcome pets, so you don't have to worry about leaving your furry friend behind. These rentals are ideal for travelers who want to bring their pets along on their vacation.

No matter which hotel, hostel, and vacation rental you choose, you'll be treated to the warm hospitality and rich culture of Budapest. From exploring the city's beautiful parks and historic landmarks to sample its delicious cuisine and vibrant nightlife, there's something for everyone in Budapest. So pack your bags and get ready to experience all that this amazing city has to offer!

Neighborhoods To Consider For Your Stay

Budapest is a vibrant and dynamic city, full of history, culture, and entertainment. It is also a city with a wide range of neighborhoods, each with its own unique character and charm. When planning a trip to Budapest, it is important to consider which neighborhood would be the best fit for your stay. Here are some of the top neighborhoods to consider for your visit to Budapest:

District V (Belváros): District V, or Belváros, is the heart of Budapest and the most popular neighborhood for tourists. It is home to many of the city's top attractions, including the Buda Castle, the Hungarian Parliament Building, and the Széchenyi

Chain Bridge. It is also a hub of shopping, dining, and entertainment, with many restaurants, cafes, and bars to choose from.

District VI (Terézváros): District VI, or Terézváros, is a trendy and fashionable neighborhood that is popular with locals and tourists alike. It is home to Andrássy Avenue, which is a UNESCO World Heritage Site and one of the city's main shopping and entertainment districts. The neighborhood is also home to the Hungarian State Opera and the famous Gerbeaud Cafe.

District VII (Erzsébetváros): District VII, or Erzsébetváros, is a lively and diverse neighborhood that is popular with artists and intellectuals. It is home to the city's Jewish Quarter, which is filled with cultural and historical sites, as well as a thriving arts scene. The neighborhood is also home to the Great Synagogue, which is the largest synagogue in Europe.

District VIII (Józsefváros): District VIII, or Józsefváros, is a diverse and multicultural neighborhood that is popular with students and young professionals. It is home to the city's main university, the Eötvös Loránd University, as well as many lively bars and cafes. The neighborhood is also home to the Hungarian National Museum, which is a must-see for history buffs.

District IX (Ferencváros): District IX, or Ferencváros, is a trendy and up-and-coming neighborhood that is popular with young professionals and families. It is home to the city's main sporting venue, the Groupama Arena, as well as many parks and green spaces. The neighborhood is also home to the Central Market Hall, which is a must-visit for foodies.

No matter which neighborhood you choose, you will find plenty of things to see and do in Budapest. Whether you are interested in history, culture, or just want to enjoy the city's lively nightlife, there is a neighborhood in Budapest that is perfect for you.

CHAPTER 5: THINGS TO DO

Buda Castle:

Buda Castle, also known as the Royal Palace, is a historic castle in Budapest, Hungary that sits atop Castle Hill on the Buda side of the Danube River. It is a major landmark in the city and a popular tourist destination.

The history of Buda Castle dates back to the 13th century, when it was first built as a royal residence for the kings of Hungary. The castle has undergone numerous renovations and expansions over the centuries, resulting in a beautiful blend of architectural styles including Gothic, Baroque, and Renaissance.

One of the main attractions of Buda Castle is the Hungarian National Gallery, which houses a collection of Hungarian art from the Middle Ages to the present day. The gallery is divided into two main sections: the Medieval and Early Modern collections, which include Gothic and Renaissance paintings, and the Modern and Contemporary collections, which showcase the work of Hungarian artists from the 19th and 20th centuries.

In addition to the Hungarian National Gallery, Buda Castle is also home to the Budapest History

Museum, which provides a comprehensive overview of the city's history. The museum features exhibits on the history of the castle, the development of the city, and the cultural and social changes that have occurred over time.

Another popular attraction at Buda Castle is the Hungarian National Library, which houses a collection of rare and valuable books and manuscripts. The library is home to over 1 million volumes, including the first book printed in Hungary and the oldest surviving Hungarian chronicle.

In addition to its museums and galleries, Buda Castle is also the official residence of the President of Hungary. Visitors can take a tour of the staterooms, where the president conducts official business and hosts official events.

One of the most striking features of Buda Castle is its location on top of Castle Hill, which provides breathtaking views of the city and the Danube River. From the castle, visitors can see all the way across the river to the Pest side of the city, and the views are particularly breathtaking at sunset.

There are several ways to get to Buda Castle, including by taking the tram or the bus. Visitors can also walk up the hill from the riverfront, which is a popular option for those who want to enjoy the beautiful surroundings.

If you're planning a trip to Budapest, a visit to Buda Castle should definitely be on your itinerary. Whether you're interested in history, art, or just want to take in the breathtaking views, this iconic castle has something for everyone.

In addition to its museums and galleries, Buda Castle is also home to a number of restaurants, cafes, and gift shops, making it a great place to spend the day. The castle is surrounded by beautiful gardens and parks, and there are several walking trails that lead from the castle down to the riverfront, providing an opportunity to explore the area further.

Overall, Buda Castle is a must-see attraction for anyone visiting Budapest. Its rich history, stunning architecture, and beautiful location make it a true gem in the city. Whether you're a history buff, art lover, or just want to take in stunning views, there is something for everyone at Buda Castle.

Hungarian Parliament:

The Hungarian Parliament, also known as the Országház, is a stunning architectural masterpiece and a must-see attraction for any visitor to Budapest. Located on the banks of the Danube River, the

Parliament is the seat of the National Assembly of Hungary and one of the oldest legislative buildings in Europe. Its ornate design, grand halls, and rich history make it a popular tourist destination, attracting over 500,000 visitors each year.

The Hungarian Parliament was built in the late 19th century, between 1885 and 1904, in the Gothic Revival style. It was designed by Imre Steindl, who won a competition held by the Hungarian government to design the new legislative building. The Parliament is an impressive example of Hungarian Art Nouveau, with a façade adorned with intricate carvings and sculptures, as well as stained glass windows and a soaring dome.

The Hungarian Parliament is a massive building, with 691 rooms, 27 gates, and 10 courtyards. It is the third largest parliament building in the world, after the U.S. Capitol and the Parliament of the United Kingdom. The building is set on a hill overlooking the Danube River, making it visible from across the city.

One of the most striking features of the Hungarian Parliament is its grand central dome, which stands 96 meters tall. The dome is topped by a crown, which is a symbol of Hungarian sovereignty. Visitors can take a tour of the Parliament, which includes a visit to the dome, where they can enjoy breathtaking views of the city from the top.

The interior of the Parliament is just as impressive as the exterior, with grand halls, ornate staircases, and intricate decorations. The main entrance is through the Kossuth Lajos tér, which is named after Lajos Kossuth, a Hungarian lawyer, journalist, politician, and Regent-President of Hungary during the Hungarian Revolution of 1848. The entrance is guarded by two statues of lions, which are symbols of Hungary.

Once inside, visitors can tour the main halls of the Parliament, including the Grand Hall, St. Stephen's

Hall, and the Hall of the National Assembly. The Grand Hall is the largest and most ornate of these, with a ceiling adorned with frescoes and a grand staircase leading to the upper levels of the building. St. Stephen's Hall is named after Saint Stephen, the first King of Hungary, and is where the coronation of the Hungarian monarchs took place. The Hall of the National Assembly is the main chamber of the Parliament, where the members of the National Assembly meet to conduct their business.

In addition to the main halls, visitors can also see the Memorial Room, which is dedicated to the victims of the 1956 Hungarian Revolution, and the Holy Crown Room, which houses the Holy Crown of

Hungary. The Holy Crown is a symbol of Hungarian statehood and was used in the coronation of Hungarian kings and queens. It is made of gold and encrusted with precious jewels and has a long and fascinating history.

Visitors to the Hungarian Parliament can also take a tour of the parliamentary gardens, which are located behind the building. The gardens feature a variety of plants and flowers, as well as a fountain and a small pond. The gardens are a peaceful oasis in the heart of the city and provide a nice respite from the hustle and bustle of downtown Budapest.

The Hungarian Parliament is open to visitors every day except for national holidays. Tours are offered in several languages, including English, German, French, and Spanish. The tours last about an hour and are led by trained guides who provide interesting and informative commentary about the history and architecture of the Parliament.

The Széchenyi Thermal Baths:

The Széchenyi Thermal Baths, also known as Széchenyi Gyógyfürdő, is a public bath complex located in the City Park of Budapest, Hungary. It is one of the largest thermal baths in Europe and a popular tourist destination for both locals and visitors to the city.

The history of the Széchenyi Thermal Baths dates back to the early 18th century when the site was used for medicinal purposes by the Turkish invaders who ruled over the region at the time. The bath complex was later expanded and modernized by the Hungarian government in the 19th and 20th centuries, and it has continued to be a popular spot for relaxation and rejuvenation ever since.

Today, the Széchenyi Thermal Baths feature a variety of indoor and outdoor pools, saunas, steam rooms, and massage rooms. The complex is divided into several different sections, each with its own unique set of facilities and amenities.

One of the most popular areas of the Széchenyi Thermal Baths is the outdoor pool complex, which features a series of interconnected pools filled with naturally heated thermal water. The temperature of the water ranges from 28 to 38 degrees Celsius, and it is rich in minerals and other therapeutic properties.

Visitors to the outdoor pool complex can enjoy a variety of activities, including swimming laps, soaking in the warm water, or lounging on the surrounding deck chairs. There are also several poolside bars and restaurants where visitors can grab a snack or a drink.

In addition to the outdoor pools, the Széchenyi Thermal Baths also feature a series of indoor pools, saunas, and steam rooms. These facilities are perfect for visitors who want to relax and unwind in a more private setting, or for those who prefer to escape the crowds during peak tourist season.

One of the most popular indoor facilities at the Széchenyi Thermal Baths is the sauna complex, which features a variety of different saunas, each with its own unique set of therapeutic properties. Some of the saunas are designed to help visitors relax and unwind, while others are meant to stimulate circulation and invigorate the body.

In addition to the saunas, the Széchenyi Thermal Baths also feature a series of steam rooms and massage rooms. These facilities are perfect for those who want to relax and rejuvenate after a long day of sightseeing or exploring the city.

The Széchenyi Thermal Baths are more than just a place to relax and unwind, however. It is also a popular spot for socializing and meeting new people. Many locals and tourists alike visit the baths on a regular basis, and it is not uncommon to see groups of friends or families enjoying the facilities together.

Aside from the pools, saunas, and massage rooms, the Széchenyi Thermal Baths also feature a number of other amenities and facilities, including a fitness center, a beauty salon, and a variety of shops and restaurants. There is also a hotel on site, which offers visitors the opportunity to stay at the baths for an extended period of time.

The Széchenyi Thermal Baths is a must-see destination for anyone visiting Budapest. It is a place where visitors can relax, unwind, and rejuvenate, while also experiencing the rich history and culture of the city. Whether you are a local or a tourist, the Széchenyi Thermal Baths is an experience that you will not want to miss.

Museum And Galleries:

Budapest, the capital city of Hungary, is a hub of culture and history. With its rich past and vibrant present, there is no shortage of museums and galleries to visit during your stay. Whether you're an art aficionado or simply looking for a way to spend a rainy afternoon, these institutions have something to offer everyone.

One of the most popular museums in Budapest is the Hungarian National Museum, which is dedicated to the history of Hungary and its people.

The museum houses a vast collection of artifacts and documents, ranging from ancient Roman relics to medieval manuscripts and modern-day art. In addition to its permanent exhibits, the museum also hosts temporary exhibitions on a variety of topics, making it a must-visit for anyone interested in Hungarian history and culture.

If you're more interested in art, the Ludwig Museum of Contemporary Art is a must-see. Located in the stunning Palace of Arts, this museum houses a collection of modern and contemporary art from around the world. From paintings and sculptures to installations and multimedia works, the Ludwig Museum has something for everyone. The museum is also home to a number of special exhibitions, workshops, and events, making it a dynamic and engaging place to visit.

Another popular museum in Budapest is the House of Terror, which is dedicated to the history of Hungary during the 20th century. Located in a former secret police headquarters, the museum tells the story of the country's tumultuous past, including its experiences under Nazi and Soviet occupation. The museum is both educational and poignant, making it a moving and important place to visit.

In addition to these larger museums, there are also many smaller galleries and cultural centers scattered throughout the city. The Open Society Archives, for example, is a research center and exhibition space that explores the history of the Cold War and its impact on Eastern Europe. The Jewish Museum is another popular destination, showcasing the history and culture of Hungary's Jewish community.

No matter what your interests are, there is something for everyone at the museums and galleries in Budapest. From ancient history to contemporary art, these institutions offer a fascinating look at the city's rich culture and past.

Traditional Hungarian Music Performance:

Traditional Hungarian music is a unique and diverse artistic tradition that has been passed down through the generations for centuries. It is an integral part of Hungarian culture and is closely tied to the country's history and folk traditions.

One of the defining characteristics of traditional Hungarian music is its use of complex and intricate melodies and rhythms. Hungarian folk music is known for its use of irregular meters and unexpected rhythmic shifts, which give it a distinct and lively sound. Many traditional Hungarian music pieces are played on a variety of instruments, including the cimbalom (a type of hammered dulcimer), the violin, the lute, and the flute.

In traditional Hungarian music performances, the emphasis is often on group participation and interaction. Folk dances are an important part of Hungarian music culture, and many traditional music performances will include group dance numbers. Dancers may perform in circles or lines, and often use hand gestures and movements to accompany the music.

Another important aspect of traditional Hungarian music is its lyrics, which often tell stories or convey cultural traditions and values. Many traditional

Hungarian songs are accompanied by lyrics that are sung in the Hungarian language, and these lyrics can be quite poetic and expressive.

Traditional Hungarian music is often performed at festivals and celebrations, as well as at more formal events such as concerts and music festivals. In recent years, there has been a resurgence of interest in traditional Hungarian music, and many young musicians and groups are dedicated to preserving and promoting this rich cultural tradition.

Overall, traditional Hungarian music is a vital and vibrant part of the country's cultural heritage, and its complex melodies and lively rhythms continue to captivate audiences both within Hungary and around the world.

Hiking In The Buda Hills:

The Buda Hills, also known as the Buda Mountains, are a range of hills located in the western part of Budapest, the capital city of Hungary. These hills offer a variety of hiking trails that cater to hikers of all skill levels, making them a popular destination for both locals and tourists alike.

One of the most popular trails in the Buda Hills is the Buda Castle Hill Funicular, which takes hikers to the top of Castle Hill, where they can enjoy panoramic views of the city. The funicular ride takes about five minutes and begins at the base of the hill, near the Buda Castle. From the top, hikers can follow the Castle Hill Circle route, which takes them past several historic landmarks, including the Buda Castle, the Matthias Church, and the Fishermen's Bastion.

Another popular trail in the Buda Hills is the Children's Railway, a narrow-gauge railway that runs through the hills and is operated by children. Hikers can ride the railway and enjoy the beautiful scenery as they pass through the forests and meadows of the hills. The railway also has several stops along the way, where hikers can disembark and explore the surrounding area.

In addition to these trails, the Buda Hills also offer a variety of more challenging routes for experienced hikers. One of the most challenging trails is the Normafa-Kopaszi Dam Circuit, which takes hikers through the forests and meadows of the hills and offers stunning views of the city. The trail is about 10 kilometers in length and takes about four hours to complete.

Regardless of which trail hikers choose, they can expect to encounter a variety of flora and fauna in the Buda Hills. The hills are home to a wide range of plants, including oak and beech trees, as well as a variety of animals, such as deer, rabbits, and foxes.

Overall, the Buda Hills are a great destination for hikers of all skill levels, offering a variety of trails that cater to everyone from beginners to experienced hikers. Whether hikers are looking for a leisurely walk or a more challenging hike, the Buda Hills have something to offer.

Taking a Boat Tour Of The Danube:

The Danube is the second-longest river in Europe and is known for its beautiful scenery and rich cultural history. Taking a boat tour of the Danube is a great way to experience this iconic river and explore the many cities and towns that line its banks.

There are many different types of boat tours available, ranging from short, leisurely cruises to longer, more in-depth tours. Some boat tours focus on the natural beauty of the river, offering opportunities to see wildlife and stunning landscapes, while others are more focused on the cultural and historical sights along the way.

One popular boat tour is the Danube Bend tour, which takes visitors on a journey through the scenic Danube Bend, where the river takes a sharp turn and flows through a series of winding valleys and cliffs. The tour typically begins in Budapest, the capital city of Hungary, and takes visitors to the towns of Visegrád, Szentendre, and Esztergom, each of which has its own unique history and character. Along the way, visitors can enjoy breathtaking views of the river and the surrounding countryside, as well as visit a variety of historical and cultural sites.

Other boat tours offer a more in-depth exploration of the Danube and its surroundings. For example, some tours take visitors on a journey down the entire length of the river, from its source in the Black Forest of Germany to its mouth in the Black Sea. These longer tours typically include stops at a variety of cities and towns along the way, allowing visitors to experience the diverse cultures and landscapes of the Danube region.

Regardless of the type of boat tour you choose, you can expect to have a memorable and enjoyable experience. Boat tours offer a unique and relaxing way to explore the Danube and its surroundings, and are a great way to learn about the rich history and culture of the region.

CHAPTER 6: FOOD AND DRINK

Traditional Hungarian Cuisine:

Traditional Hungarian cuisine is known for its rich and flavorful dishes, many of which are influenced by the country's central European and Eastern European heritage. Some of the most popular and well-known dishes in Hungarian cuisine include goulash, a hearty stew made with beef, potatoes, and spices; chicken paprikash, a dish made with chicken, paprika, and sour cream; and lángos, a type of deep-fried dough topped with cheese, sour cream, and other toppings.

Other popular dishes in Hungarian cuisine include töltött káposzta, which is stuffed cabbage rolls filled with meat and rice; halászlé, a spicy fish soup; and túrógombóc, dumplings filled with curd cheese and served with a sweet vanilla sauce.

Hungarian cuisine also has a strong tradition of baked goods, including pastries, bread, and cakes. Some popular baked goods include strudel, a flaky pastry filled with fruit or other sweet fillings; kürtőskalács, a spiral-shaped pastry coated in sugar and baked over an open fire; and somlói Galuska, a layered cake with chocolate, whipped cream, and rum-soaked sponges.

To find traditional Hungarian cuisine, you can visit restaurants or cafes in Hungary or in areas with a significant Hungarian population, such as parts of Austria, Serbia, and Romania. Many cities in the United States, including New York and Chicago, also have Hungarian restaurants and bakeries where you can try traditional dishes and baked goods.

It's worth noting that Hungarian cuisine can vary by region and by individual recipe, so the dishes you find at a Hungarian restaurant or cafe may vary from one place to another. However, most traditional Hungarian cuisine features bold flavors, hearty ingredients, and a mix of sweet and savory elements, making it a unique and satisfying dining experience

Restaurants And Cafes:

Budapest is the capital and largest city of Hungary, known for its rich history, culture, and stunning architecture. The city is also home to a diverse range of restaurants and cafes, offering a wide variety of cuisines and dining experiences for visitors and locals alike. In this book, we will explore some of the best restaurants and cafes in Budapest, from traditional Hungarian cuisine to international flavors and everything in between.

One of the most iconic and popular types of dining establishments in Budapest is the traditional Hungarian tavern, or "csárda." These rustic restaurants, often located in the countryside or in the city's historic districts, serve hearty and flavorful Hungarian dishes such as goulash, pork knuckle, and chicken paprikash. Some of the best csárdas in Budapest include Kéhli Csárda, Élesztő Csárda, and Bécsi Szelet Csárda.

If you're in the mood for international cuisine, Budapest has no shortage of options. The city is home to a wide range of international restaurants, including Italian, Thai, Chinese, and more. Some popular international restaurants in Budapest include Trattoria Toscana, Thai Elephant, and Shambala.

For a more casual dining experience, Budapest has a thriving cafe culture. The city is home to numerous coffee shops and cafes, ranging from traditional Hungarian coffee houses to modern specialty coffee shops. Some popular cafes in Budapest include New York Cafe, Central Cafe, and Szatyor Kávéház.

In addition to traditional sit-down restaurants and cafes, Budapest also has a vibrant street food scene. The city is home to numerous food markets, food trucks, and street vendors selling a wide range of dishes, from hearty sandwiches and soups to sweet pastries and desserts. Some popular street food options in Budapest include lángos (deep-fried dough topped with cheese and sour cream), chimney cakes (spiral-shaped pastries rolled in sugar and spices), and kürtőskalács (sweet, spiral-shaped pastries baked over an open fire).

No matter what type of dining experience you're looking for, Budapest has something for everyone. From traditional Hungarian taverns to international cuisine and casual cafes, the city offers a wide range of dining options to suit every taste and budget. So whether you're a foodie or just looking for a casual meal, you're sure to find something to enjoy in Budapest.

Nightlife Options, Including Bars And Clubs:

If you're looking for a place to grab a drink and socialize, Budapest has a range of bars that cater to all types of people. For a classic Hungarian experience, visit a "ruin bar," which are repurposed abandoned buildings turned into bars. These bars are known for their unique and quirky decor and are popular among locals and tourists alike. Some popular ruin bars in Budapest include Szimpla Kert, Instant, and Fogasház.

If you're in the mood for a more upscale bar experience, Budapest also has a number of trendy cocktail bars. These bars often have a chic atmosphere and serve a variety of creative cocktails. Some popular cocktail bars in Budapest include Bar 360, The London Cocktail Club, and Apothecary.

For those who enjoy live music, Budapest has a number of bars and clubs that feature live bands and DJs. These venues range from small and intimate to large and lively and offer a variety of musical genres, including jazz, rock, and electronic music. Some popular live music venues in Budapest include the A38 Ship, the Budapest Jazz Club, and the Dürer Kert.

If you're in the mood to dance, Budapest has a number of clubs that stay open until the early hours of the morning. These clubs often feature international DJs and a variety of music genres, including house, techno, and hip-hop. Some popular clubs in Budapest include the Laugardagskvöld, the Akvárium Klub, and the Flex Club.

In addition to the traditional bars and clubs, Budapest also has a number of unique nightlife experiences to offer. For example, the city has several thermal baths that are open late and offer a chance to relax and unwind after a night out. The Széchenyi Thermal Bath and the Rudas Thermal Bath are both popular options.

No matter what your preferences are, Budapest has something to offer for everyone looking to experience the city's nightlife. Whether you're looking for a cozy bar to grab a drink, a lively club to dance the night away, or a unique experience like a thermal bath, Budapest has it all

CHAPTER 7: SHOPPING

Budapest is a city known for its rich history and cultural traditions, and one of the best ways to immerse yourself in the local culture is by visiting the city's local markets and souvenir shops.

One of the most popular markets in Budapest is the Great Market Hall, located in the city center. This market, also known as the Central Market Hall, is a three-story building that features a wide variety of stalls selling fresh produce, meats, cheeses, and other local products. It is a great place to try traditional Hungarian dishes like goulash and langos, and to purchase souvenirs such as handmade crafts, traditional clothing, and folk art.

Another popular market in Budapest is the Ecseri Flea Market, located on the outskirts of the city. This market is known for its vast selection of antique and vintage items, including furniture, clothing, and collectibles. It is a great place to find unique souvenirs and get a feel for the city's history.

In addition to markets, Budapest also has a number of souvenir shops scattered throughout the city. These shops often sell a variety of traditional Hungarian products, such as hand-painted ceramics, embroidered linens, and jewelry. Many of these souvenir shops also sell local food products, such as paprika and other spices, honey, and liqueurs.

If you're looking for more modern souvenirs, Budapest also has a number of gift shops that sell items such as t-shirts, magnets, and other tourist trinkets. These shops can be found throughout the city, including in popular tourist areas like Vaciutca and the Buda Castle District.

No matter what type of souvenir you're looking for, Budapest has a wide variety of options to choose from. Whether you're interested in traditional crafts or more modern gifts, you're sure to find something to take home as a reminder of your trip to this beautiful city.

High-End Boutiques And Department Stores:

Budapest is a city that offers a range of shopping options, including high-end boutiques and department stores. These stores are located throughout the city and offer a wide selection of luxury goods and designer brands.

One of the most popular high-end department stores in Budapest is the Andrássy út location of the Hungarian chain store, Árkád. This store is located in the heart of the city and offers a wide range of luxury brands, including Prada, Gucci, and Versace.

The store also has a large selection of designer clothing, accessories, and beauty products.

Another popular high-end department store in Budapest is the Fény Street location of the Hungarian chain store, Corvin. This store is located in the city center and offers a wide range of luxury brands, including Chanel, Dior, and Louis Vuitton. The store also has a large selection of designer clothing, accessories, and beauty products.

In addition to department stores, Budapest also has a number of high-end boutiques scattered throughout the city. These boutiques often specialize in specific types of products, such as clothing, accessories, or beauty products. Some popular high-end boutiques in Budapest include the Hungarian chain store, Zara, and the Italian chain store, Benetton.

If you're looking for a more unique shopping experience, Budapest also has a number of independent boutiques that offer a range of designer brands and locally made products. These boutiques are often located in the city's more trendy neighborhoods, such as the Jewish Quarter and the Buda Castle District.

No matter what you're looking for, Budapest has a range of high-end shopping options to choose from.

Whether you're interested in luxury brands or unique, locally-made products, you're sure to find something to suit your taste in this vibrant city.

CHAPTER 8: DAY TRIPS FROM BUDAPEST

Szentendre:

Szentendre is a charming town located just a short distance from Budapest, the capital city of Hungary. Known for its colorful houses, winding streets, and rich history, Szentendre is a popular destination for tourists and locals alike.

One of the best ways to experience Szentendre is to take an excursion from Budapest. Many tour companies offer half-day or full-day trips to the town, which typically include round-trip transportation and guided tours of the main attractions.

One of the highlights of a visit to Szentendre is the opportunity to explore the town's narrow streets and alleyways, which are lined with beautifully preserved houses in a variety of colors. Many of these houses date back to the 18th and 19th centuries and were built in the Baroque and Rococo styles. Some of the most picturesque streets in Szentendre include Kossuth Lajos, Fő, and Szerb utca.

Another must-see attraction in Szentendre is the Serbian Orthodox Church, also known as the

Church of St. John the Baptist. This beautifully decorated church was built in the early 18th century and is one of the most important religious landmarks in Hungary. Visitors can take a guided tour of the church to learn about its history and admire its ornate frescoes and icons.

In addition to its charming streets and historic landmarks, Szentendre is also home to a number of museums and galleries. The Margit Kovacs Ceramics Museum is a popular destination for art lovers, featuring a collection of ceramics by the famous Hungarian artist Margit Kovacs. The Vasarely Museum is another notable attraction, showcasing the works of Op Art pioneer Victor Vasarely.

After exploring the sights and sounds of Szentendre, visitors can take a break at one of the town's many cafes or restaurants. Szentendre is known for its delicious food, including traditional Hungarian dishes like goulash and strudel. Many of the town's restaurants offer outdoor seating, allowing visitors to enjoy their meals in the charming surroundings of Szentendre's streets and squares.

Overall, an excursion to Szentendre is a must-do for anyone visiting Budapest. With its charming streets, historic landmarks, and delicious food, Szentendre is the perfect escape from the bustle of the city and offers a unique and authentic Hungarian experience.

Excursions To Visegrád:

Visegrád is a small town located in Hungary, just a short distance from Budapest. Known for its castle, stunning views, and rich history, Visegrád is a popular destination for tourists and locals alike.

One of the best ways to experience Visegrád is to take an excursion from Budapest. Many tour companies offer half-day or full-day trips to the town, which typically include round-trip transportation and guided tours of the main attractions.

One of the highlights of a visit to Visegrád is the opportunity to explore the Visegrád Castle, also known as the Royal Palace. This castle was once the residence of Hungarian kings and is now a popular tourist attraction. Visitors can take a guided tour of the castle to learn about its history and admire its stunning architecture. The castle is located on top of a hill and offers breathtaking views of the surrounding countryside.

In addition to the castle, Visegrád is also home to a number of other attractions. The Citadel, also known as the Citadel of Visegrád, is a well-preserved fortification that was built in the 14th century. Visitors can take a guided tour of the Citadel to learn about its history and admire its impressive walls and towers.

After exploring the sights and sounds of Visegrád, visitors can take a break at one of the town's many cafes or restaurants. Visegrád is known for its delicious food, including traditional Hungarian dishes like goulash and strudel. Many of the town's restaurants offer outdoor seating, allowing visitors to enjoy their meals in the charming surroundings of Visegrád's streets and squares.

Overall, an excursion to Visegrád is a must-do for anyone visiting Budapest. With its stunning castle, breathtaking views, and rich history, Visegrád is the perfect escape from the bustle of the city and offers a unique and authentic Hungarian experience.

Danube Bend:

The Danube Bend is a scenic region in Hungary located about 40 miles northwest of Budapest. It is known for its natural beauty, historical landmarks, and cultural significance. The Danube River, which flows through the region, is the second-longest river in Europe and has played a central role in the history of the Danube Bend.

The earliest recorded history of the Danube Bend dates back to the Neolithic era, when the region was settled by various tribes and cultures. In the Bronze Age, the region was inhabited by the Celts, who built fortifications and settlements along the river.

During the Roman Empire, the Danube Bend became an important trade route and was heavily fortified to defend against invasions. The Romans built several military camps and fortifications in the region, including the famous Hadrian's Wall in England.

In the Middle Ages, the Danube Bend was a center of trade and commerce. The region was also home to many monasteries and castles, which were built by the ruling nobles to protect their lands and wealth.

In the modern era, the Danube Bend has continued to be an important region for trade and tourism. The region is home to several major cities, including Budapest, the capital of Hungary, and Szentendre, a popular tourist destination known for its art and architecture.

The Danube Bend is also home to several historical landmarks, including the ruins of the Roman fortification of Aquincum, the medieval castle of Visegrád, and the Baroque-style Esztergom Basilica.

Today, the Danube Bend is a popular destination for tourists from all over the world, who come to experience the region's rich history, cultural heritage, and natural beauty

Gellért Hill Cave:

Gellért Hill is a hill in Budapest, Hungary, located on the Buda side of the city. The hill is named after Saint Gerard, a missionary who was martyred in the area in the 10th century. One of the main attractions on Gellért Hill is the Gellért Hill Cave, a series of underground caves and tunnels that have a rich history dating back thousands of years.

The Gellért Hill Cave is believed to have been formed around 70 million years ago, during the Cretaceous period. The cave was formed by the movement of underground water, which carved out the tunnels and chambers over time.

In the Middle Ages, the Gellért Hill Cave was used by the monks of the Pauline Order as a place of meditation and retreat. The cave was also used as a shelter during times of war and as a hiding place for treasure.

In the 19th century, the Gellért Hill Cave was rediscovered and became a popular tourist attraction. In the early 20th century, the cave was extensively explored and mapped, and a series of staircases and walkways were built to allow visitors to explore the cave more easily.

Today, the Gellért Hill Cave is a popular tourist destination in Budapest, attracting visitors from all over the world. The cave is open to the public and can be accessed through a series of staircases and walkways. Visitors can explore the cave's various chambers and see the underground lake, which is home to a colony of bats. The cave is also home to several species of cave-dwelling animals, including cave salamanders, which are native to the region.

CHAPTER 9: PRACTICAL INFORMATION

Budapest, the capital and largest city of Hungary, is a popular tourist destination known for its rich history, cultural attractions, and beautiful architecture. If you are planning a trip to Budapest, it is important to consider your budget and how to manage your money while you are there. Here are some tips to help you manage your currency and budget while you are in Budapest:

Know The Local Currency: The official currency of Hungary is the Hungarian forint (HUF). It is important to familiarize yourself with the exchange rate and be able to convert prices to your home currency. This will help you to budget effectively and avoid overspending. You can find the current exchange rate online or at a currency exchange office.

Get Cash Before You Arrive: It is a good idea to get some cash in Hungarian forints before you arrive in Budapest. This will allow you to pay for small expenses and get around the city more easily. You can exchange your home currency for forints at a currency exchange office or at the airport upon arrival. Keep in mind that currency exchange rates can vary, so it is a good idea to shop around to get the best deal.

Use ATMs: ATMs are widely available in Budapest and are a convenient way to get cash while you are there. Just be aware of any fees that may be charged by your bank or the ATM operator. It is also a good idea to inform your bank before you travel, as some banks may block foreign transactions as a security measure.

Use a credit card: Credit cards are widely accepted in Budapest, and using one can be a convenient and secure way to pay for goods and services. Just be sure to check with your credit card issuer to see if there are any fees for foreign transactions or cash advances.

Keep Track Of Your Spending: It is important to keep track of your spending while you are in Budapest to make sure you stay within your budget. Use a budget planner or app to help you keep track of your expenses and make sure you are not overspending.

Take advantage of free activities: There are many free or low-cost activities to enjoy in Budapest, such as visiting the city's many parks and gardens, walking along the Danube River, or exploring the city's many museums and galleries. Taking advantage of these free activities can help you to save money and stay within your budget.

Consider staying in budget-friendly accommodation: There are many budget-friendly accommodation options in Budapest, such as hostels or Airbnb rentals. Doing your research and comparing prices can help you to find the best deal and stay within your budget.

By following these tips, you can effectively manage your currency and budget while you are in Budapest and make the most of your trip.

Communication And Language:

Communication and language can be important considerations when traveling to Budapest, as the city is located in a foreign country where the primary language is Hungarian. Here are some tips to help you communicate and navigate language barriers while you are in Budapest:

Learn some basic phrases: It is always helpful to know a few basic phrases in the local language, such as "hello," "please," and "thank you." Even a small effort to communicate in the local language can go a long way in terms of building goodwill and showing respect to the local culture. You can find online resources or a language-learning app to help you learn some basic phrases in Hungarian.

Bring a phrasebook or use a translation app: If you are not confident in your language skills, you can bring a phrasebook or use a translation app to help you communicate while you are in Budapest. There are many language translation apps available that can help you to translate words and phrases in real time, or you can use them to type out a longer message.

Use body language and gestures: Even if you do not speak the local language, you can still communicate effectively by using body language and gestures. Smiling, nodding, and pointing can all be useful ways to convey meaning and get your message across.

Look for places that cater to tourists: Many restaurants, shops, and other businesses in Budapest cater to tourists and may have staff who speak English or other languages. Look for these places if you need to communicate with someone and are not comfortable using the local language.

Hire a translator or guide: If you are traveling to Budapest on a business trip or for another specific purpose, you may want to consider hiring a translator or guide to help you communicate and navigate the city. This can be especially helpful if you are attending meetings or events where language skills are necessary.

By following these tips, you can effectively communicate and navigate language barriers while you are in Budapest. It is always a good idea to be respectful and patient when communicating with people in a foreign country and to remember that language barrier can be challenging for everyone.

Health And Safety Advice:

Budapest is a generally safe city, but like any destination, it is important to be aware of your surroundings and take steps to ensure your health and safety while you are there. Here are some tips to help you stay safe and healthy while you are in Budapest:

Research Your Destination: Before you travel, it is a good idea to research your destination and familiarize yourself with any potential health or safety risks. This can help you to make informed decisions about your travel plans and take appropriate precautions.

Get Travel Insurance: Travel insurance can provide peace of mind and help you to cope with unexpected situations, such as trip cancellations, medical emergencies, and lost or stolen property. It is a good idea to research and compare different travel insurance policies to find one that meets your needs.

Stay hydrated: Hungary can be hot and dry in the summer, and it is important to stay hydrated by drinking plenty of water. Carry a water bottle with you and refill it as needed to stay hydrated throughout the day.

Protect Yourself From The Sun: The sun in Hungary can be strong, especially in the summer months. Wear sunscreen and a hat, and try to stay in the shade as much as possible to protect your skin from the sun's harmful rays.

Be Aware Of Pickpockets: Like any major city, Budapest has its share of pickpockets. Be aware of your surroundings and keep your valuables safe by keeping your bags and pockets close to your body and avoiding crowded areas.

Know Where To Find Medical Care: In case of a medical emergency, it is important to know where to find medical care. Most hotels and hostels can provide information on local hospitals and clinics, or you can ask a local for recommendations. It is also a good idea to bring a copy of your insurance policy and any necessary medications with you while you travel.

By following these tips, you can stay safe and healthy while you are in Budapest. It is always a good idea to be aware of your surroundings and take appropriate precautions to protect yourself and your belongings while you are traveling.

CHAPTER 10: CONCLUSION AND FINAL THOUGHTS

Budapest, the capital of Hungary, is a city with a rich history and culture that spans over 2,000 years. Located along the banks of the Danube River, Budapest is a city that is known for its stunning architecture, delicious cuisine, and vibrant nightlife.

One of the highlights of a trip to Budapest is the opportunity to explore its historic castles and Landmarks. The Buda Castle, located on Castle Hill in Buda, is a must-see attraction. The castle dates back to the 13th century and is home to the

Hungarian National Gallery and the Budapest History Museum.

Another popular landmark in Budapest is the Széchenyi Chain Bridge, which spans the Danube River and connects Buda and Pest. The bridge was the first permanent bridge to be built across the Danube and is a symbol of the city.

For those interested in experiencing the city's cultural side, a visit to the Hungarian State Opera House is a must. The opera house is home to the Hungarian National Ballet and the Hungarian National Opera and offers a variety of performances throughout the year.

Foodies will also enjoy a trip to Budapest, as the city is known for its delicious cuisine. Traditional dishes include goulash, a hearty meat stew served with potatoes and vegetables, and strudel, a sweet pastry filled with fruit or cheese.

Budapest is also a city that is known for its vibrant nightlife. The city has a variety of clubs and bars that stay open late, making it a great destination for those who love to party.

Overall, a trip to Budapest is a unique and memorable experience. From its historic landmarks and cultural attractions to its delicious cuisine and lively nightlife, there is something for everyone in this beautiful city.

Suggestions for extending your stay or planning a return visit.

If you're planning a trip to Budapest and want to extend your stay or are considering planning a return visit, there are plenty of things to do and see in the city.

One suggestion is to explore the city's many museums and galleries. Budapest is home to a number of museums and galleries that showcase the city's rich history and culture, including the Hungarian National Gallery, the Museum of Fine Arts, and the Holocaust Memorial Center.

Another suggestion is to take a walk along the Danube River, which runs through the city. Along the way, you can visit iconic landmarks such as the Buda Castle, the Széchenyi Chain Bridge, and the Fisherman's Bastion.

For those interested in experiencing the city's culinary scene, there are many restaurants and cafes to choose from. From traditional Hungarian dishes to international cuisine, there is something for every taste. Don't forget to try some of the local wine and craft beer as well.

If you're looking for some relaxation and rejuvenation, Budapest is also home to a number of thermal baths. The Széchenyi Thermal Bath, located in the city center, is a popular choice. The baths are open year-round and offer a variety of treatments and therapies.

Finally, don't miss the opportunity to experience the city's vibrant nightlife. Budapest is known for its clubs and bars, which stay open late and offer a variety of music and entertainment.

Overall, there are many options for extending your stay or planning a return visit to Budapest. From its museums and galleries to its delicious cuisine and lively nightlife, there is something for everyone in this beautiful city.